*V*isiting the *P*ast

Shakespeare's Birthplace

Jane Shuter

www.heinemann.co.uk/library
Visit our website to find out more information about Heinemann Library books.

To order:
☎ Phone 44 (0) 1865 888066
 Send a fax to 44 (0) 1865 314091
 Visit the Heinemann Bookshop at www.heinemann.co.uk/library to browse our catalogue and order online.

First published in Great Britain by Heinemann Library, Halley Court, Jordan Hill, Oxford
OX2 8EJ, a division of Reed Educational and Professional Publishing Ltd. Heinemann
is a registered trademark of Reed Educational & Professional Publishing Ltd.

OXFORD MELBOURNE AUCKLAND JOHANNESBURG BLANTYRE
GABORONE IBADAN PORTSMOUTH NH (USA) CHICAGO

Designed by Visual Image
Illustrations by Paul Bale and Jane Durston
Originated by Ambassador Litho Ltd
Printed by Wing King Tong in Hong Kong/China

ISBN 0 431 02785 4
06 05 04 03 02
10 9 8 7 6 5 4 3 2 1

British Library Cataloguing in Publication Data

Shuter, Jane
Shakespeare's birthplace. – (Visiting the past)
1. Shakespeare, William, 1564–1616 – Birthplace – Juvenile literature
    2. Shakespeare, William, 1564–1616 – Homes and haunts – England –
    Stratford-upon-Avon – Juvenile literature
I. Title
823.3'3

Acknowledgements

The publishers would like to thank Trevor Clifford for permission to reproduce all photographs with the exception of
the photograph on p.4 for which we thank The Shakespeare Centre.

Thanks to Sarah Jervis and all at the Shakespeare Birthplace Trust for their help with the photographs.

Cover photograph reproduced with permission of Trevor Clifford.

The publishers would like to thank Dr Paul Edmondson, Head of Education at the Shakespeare Birthplace Trust, for his
comments during the preparation of this book.

Every effort has been made to contact copyright holders of any material reproduced in this book.
Any omissions will be rectified in subsequent printings if notice is given to the Publishers.

Any words appearing in the text in bold, **like this**, are explained in the Glossary.

Contents

Shakespeare's Birthplace

William Shakespeare, born in April 1564, was the son of John and Mary Shakespeare. John was a **glover**, making and selling gloves and other leather goods, such as purses and belts, from his workshop in the family home. William Shakespeare was born at a time when the skills of reading and writing became more important and more widespread. Neither John nor Mary could write, but they almost certainly sent their sons to Stratford Grammar School.

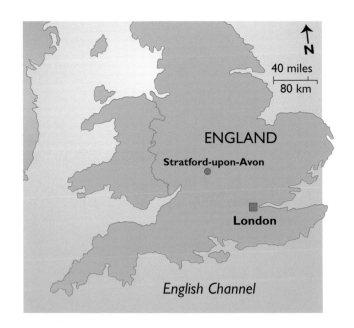

Certainly William learned to read and write somewhere and he also learned to love acting and plays. The first recorded appearance of actors in Stratford was in 1569, when John Shakespeare was mayor. When he was about 22, William Shakespeare went to London and joined a group of actors working in the theatres there. He went on to become the most famous **playwright** in history, one whose plays are still performed worldwide today.

This painting is called the 'Ely Palace' portrait and is thought by some to show William Shakespeare. There is no portrait from the time that definitely shows Shakespeare.

4

Shakespeare's Birthplace has been restored by the Shakespeare Birthplace Trust so that the outside looks very much as it did when he lived there. The street, however, looks very different! It is paved and closed to traffic, whereas in Shakespeare's time it would have been covered with an uneven stone surface at best and full of people, carts and even animals and rubbish.

Shakespeare's Birthplace, in Stratford upon Avon, is one of the few **Tudor** houses that belonged to an ordinary family that has been preserved much as it was at the time. The Birthplace shows what ordinary homes were like, and how they were built and furnished. It also gives an idea of how people lived and worked at the time. Since 1847 the house has been cared for by the Shakespeare Birthplace Trust, because it was the place where William Shakespeare was born and grew up. Some rooms contain original furniture and decoration from the time, others have been recreated to show us what life was like in Shakespeare's age.

The Shakespeare Birthplace Trust also cares for four other houses connected with William Shakespeare in Stratford and the surrounding area. This is Hall's Croft, which was the home of Dr John Hall, who married Shakespeare's daughter, Susanna, in 1607.

Shakespeare's Stratford

Stratford was a market town with about 1500 people living in it. As the largest town in the area, it had a market every Thursday. Here local farmers and **craftsmen** sold their produce, from butter and eggs to cattle and sheep. Glove-making was one of the most important trades in the town.

The town council had strict rules about how the markets should be run and made sure that shoppers were not being cheated. It set prices, checked measuring equipment and checked the quality of food for sale. For instance, butter, cream and beer, all sold at market, went bad easily. The council appointed people to sample these things, to make sure only 'wholesome' foods were sold. One of John Shakespeare's first jobs for the council (he eventually became mayor) was as a beer taster.

This house, called Nash's House, belonged to Thomas Nash, who married one of Shakespeare's granddaughters. Like all the buildings in Stratford, apart from the two most important churches, it was built from wood. This meant there was always a serious risk of fire. In 1594 and 1595 there were two fires that destroyed about 200 houses in Stratford.

This is the Grammar School that William Shakespeare and his brother probably attended. It was set up in 1553, paid for by money left to it by people when they died. The school was set up at a time when many towns all over the country set up schools for the first time. These schools only took local boys, not girls.

Tudor builders at work.

Building the house

Palaces and homes of rich **nobles** were built from whatever the ruler or noble wanted and could afford. The homes of most other people were built from local building materials. In the Stratford area wood was one of the most plentiful building materials, so ordinary homes were made mainly of wood.

The builders of the Birthplace first laid a stone base which rose about 90 centimetres above the ground. The stone came from a quarry in nearby Wilmcote. On top of this, carpenters built a frame for the house, using oak beams of various thicknesses, depending on the weight the beams had to carry. The wood came from the nearby Forest of Arden. The beams were fixed together using wooden pegs. Wood was more expensive than the materials used to fill the gaps between the beams, so the closer together the beams of wood are in a frame house, the more expensive it was to build and the richer the original owners were – the cost of the Birthplace was average for its time.

This is the stone base that the wooden frame of the Birthplace was built on. There are three sets of pegs shown in the photo, each set holds an upright beam to the beam that is resting on the stone base.

The beams used to build the Birthplace vary in thickness. The thickest of the upright ones support the corners of the house. The thickest beams that run across the house are the ones that support the boards for the floors of the upstairs rooms. The guttering in the photo above is modern – houses in Shakespeare's time did not have gutters.

Wattle and daub

The gaps between the beams were filled with **wattle and daub**. First, flexible sticks were woven to make panels of the right size, which were fitted into place. These were then covered in a layer of mud and straw, called daub. This could also be made with mud and hair, or dried grasses – anything that was free or cheap locally and gave the mud texture. Once this rough layer had dried off, the surface was plastered over with a finer, smooth, plaster. Unlike daub, which was made from local materials, plaster had to be bought and needed a skilled plasterer to get a good finish.

The photo shows some wattle and daub, covered with a sheet of modern glass to protect it.

The roof

The roof of the Birthplace was made as part of the timber framework. It was almost certainly boarded right across. This was probably first covered with a layer of straw thatch, then by clay tiles.

Windows

The frames for the windows of **Tudor** homes were made from wood, built as part of the frame of the house. The earliest windows of the Birthplace were probably just an opening covered by a wooden shutter. The smaller window (a) is part of the original building, and probably just had a shutter at first. Windows were later filled in with pieces of polished animal horn, usually cow horn. The horn was soaked until it could be flattened and then cut into thin sheets. Sometimes glass was used, but it was expensive. The pieces of horn or glass were fixed together with strips of lead. The bottom window (b) was bigger and put in later, when glass was cheaper.

Finishing off

The next stage in house building was the finishing off, done once the roof, walls and windows were finished and the inside of the house was weatherproof. Finishing off was providing the floors, fireplaces, doors and other equipment that made the house ready to move into.

Fireplaces

Fireplaces were built to heat the house and to cook with. The chimneystacks were also built of Wilmcote stone. Each room in the family house had a fireplace, although only the kitchen was likely to have a fire lit at all times. The workshop was unheated. This was usual at the time.

This is the fireplace in the hall. The ledge on the far side, where the jugs are, was used for storage or sitting on in cold weather.

The floor of the hall had stone paving.

Floors

The downstairs floors were covered with flat stone paving. The stone stopped the damp creeping up from the earth below. Wooden floors would have rotted if they were in contact with the earth, so wooden floors needed more complicated foundations. Stone slabs were simple, cheap and easy to keep clean. The upstairs floors, and the stairs leading up, were made from wood planks nailed to support beams running in the opposite direction to the planks.

Candles were used for lighting. Lanterns like this one were sometimes used indoors, but were most often used outside, where the wind would blow out an unprotected flame.

Water and sewage

Ordinary homes in **Tudor** times did not have running water, drains or **sewers**. Water was fetched from an outside well, bucketful by bucketful. This water was used for washing, cooking, washing-up and for various leather-working jobs in the workshop. Dirty water was thrown into the garden, or onto the street.

The Birthplace had no toilet. Because urine was used in the leatherworking process, it is likely the Shakespeares collected up their urine into a barrel in the yard. Other waste was put onto authorized 'muckheaps'. You could be fined for not using them – John Shakespeare was. In Tudor times few ordinary homes had toilets. Homes that did have toilets mostly drained the sewage into an underground pit (emptied regularly), or ran it through a drain hole directly onto the street. If their homes were built near, or over a stream or river, they drained the sewage to that instead.

Doors and window shutters were made to fit the openings made when the frame of the house was built. They were fixed to the frames with iron hinges.

11

Decoration

Once the house was built it could be decorated and furnished. The first stage in the decorating process was to cover the walls and ceilings inside with a coat of **limewash**, which dried white. This made the low, darkish rooms lighter, by reflecting back what light there was. It was also a good protective coating for the wood.

Wall hangings

Almost all the walls of the house were then covered with wall hangings called 'painted cloths'. The workshop, kitchen and storage rooms would not have had wall hangings, but the main living rooms and bedrooms would have. Hangings were a sign of importance, poorer families would not have had them.

Wall hangings were sheets of **linen** cloth that were painted with a gluey mixture called **size** to stiffen them. They were then cut to fit the shape of the room, so that they fitted around the door and window frames and hung from ceiling to floor. They were then fitted to the walls, rather like loose modern wallpaper. Once this was done, the wall hangings were painted, with bright colours and patterns.

The wall hangings shown here are modern reproductions, made using techniques and patterns that were used in Shakespeare's time. They hang in the hall, **parlour** and the main bedroom. The photo shows how the hangings were shaped around door and window frames.

Tudor windows were small and often had shutters, occasionally they had a single curtain. The Tudors put curtains around their beds. Once the fire had died out for the night, if there was a fire in the bedroom at all, bedrooms could get very cold. Good thick curtains all around and over the top of the bed made a kind of tent to keep the heat in.

Tapestries

Tapestries were sometimes hung on the walls of **Tudor** homes. These were different from wall hangings and were used in the way that many people use paintings or posters today. They were usually square or rectangular and were seldom more than a few feet across in an ordinary home. Poor people did not have tapestries at all, while the rich often had very complicated ones that covered a whole wall. They were woven using coloured wools to create a picture.

Cushions and curtains

Tudor furniture was rather hard and uncomfortable, so the women of the house often made cushions. They were stuffed mainly with wool, but sometimes with horsehair or feathers, to make sitting down more comfortable. The patterned cushions were woven using linen and woollen thread.

Furniture

Tudor homes had far less furniture than modern homes. People had fewer possessions generally, so they needed less storage space for clothes, bedding and cooking and eating equipment. People did not replace their furniture often, either. Indeed, many pieces of furniture in a Tudor home were passed down from parents or grandparents.

Most ordinary homes had a dining table in the hall big enough for the household to sit around, and just enough chairs and benches for everyone to sit down. These hard, wooden chairs, benches and stools would have been the only seating in the house. Soft, stuffed furniture, such as sofas and armchairs, did not exist. Cushions were the only way of making the seats more comfortable.

The **parlour** of the Birthplace would have been seen as comfortable at the time, even though there is only a rush mat on the stone floor and the chair and stool are wooden. There is a chest at the foot of the bed, for storing things that needed keeping safe. The case on the table would have been used to store valuables, like money. Other possessions were stored on the mantelpiece over the fireplace.

Most homes also had a dresser for various plates, bowls, dishes and mugs. An ordinary home often had several chests, upstairs and downstairs. They were used for storing clothes, bedding and anything else that needed to be kept safe from mice, rats, moths and other creatures that might damage them.

Beds

In a Tudor household the head of the household and his wife slept in the best bed in the house. In a family like the Shakespeares this meant a four-poster bed with hangings.

Many four-poster beds had a smaller wooden bed frame tucked under them, called a 'truckle bed'. This bed was pulled out at night for the youngest children to sleep on.

The rope base could sag badly as the rope stretched. It needed tightening up from time to time, using a wooden tool. The phrase 'sleep tight' is thought to come from the fact that a tight rope base is more comfortable to sleep on.

Beds were made from a wooden frame. The mattress and bedding were supported on a rope base that was threaded up and down, and side to side across the frame. A plaited rush mat on top of it helped to provide support, too.

Food

Food and flavouring

Many families grew their own fruit and vegetables. Ordinary **Tudor** gardens were carefully laid out to make the most of the space and the plants. Fruit trees were trained along garden walls, so as not to take up too much space. Vegetables were grown mixed in with flowers known to repel the pests that could damage the vegetables. Many flowers were used to cook with, too. Roses and violets were most often used for flavouring food.

Families often kept animals in their gardens, too. Chickens were useful for both eggs and, when they stopped laying enough eggs, meat. A family, or a group of families, might also keep a pig, even in towns. Pigs were useful because they could be fed on household scraps. When they were killed, in the autumn, the meat could be used in many ways. Much of it was eaten fresh, but it could also be salted, turned into sausages and smoked as ham and bacon.

Meat, fish, butter, cheese and eggs were usually bought at market. Wild game (rabbits, hare and deer) were also eaten.

One of the commonest meals was a soup called 'pottage', where everything was cooked in one big iron pot hung over the fire. The hook that the pot is hanging from could be raised or lowered, to move the pot closer to the fire, or further away. Pottage did not have an exact cooking time, but could be put on first thing in the morning and left cooking until people wanted to eat.

Cooking

All cooking was done over an open fire, but a wide range of cookery was done by adjusting the heat of the fire and using a variety of cooking containers. So something could be cooked at a high heat over the main part of the fire, while a different dish could be cooked slowly on a bed of coals raked out of the main fire – this would be left slowly smouldering.

Roasting

Meat was roasted on a high heat. It was usually roasted in a piece large enough to fit onto a long, large metal skewer called a **spit**. The spit stood at the front of the fire and often had a handle to turn, so that the meat could be cooked evenly on all sides. A metal pan was put under the roasting meat to catch the fat that dripped off it. Vegetables were usually boiled, buttered or eaten as salads, not roasted.

The household

A household is everyone who lives in the same house. In **Tudor** times, households were organized into levels of importance and everyone had to behave in the right way for their position in the household. The most important member of the household was the head of the household. In Shakespeare's Birthplace the head of the household was John Shakespeare. Everyone had to obey him, but in return he had to look after everyone in the household. In 1570, when William Shakespeare was six, there were about nine people in the household.

The family

The rest of the family came after John Shakespeare in importance. Mary, John's wife, was next in importance after him, followed by the children. Among the children the boys came first, in order of age – William then Gilbert. The girls were last, again in order of age, Joan then Anne.

A person's place in the household was obvious everywhere. So at meals the head of the household sat at the top end of the table. He had the only chair with arms. His wife sat opposite him at the other end. The rest of the family sat along the sides, on benches or various stools. In some families, where there were not enough chairs for everyone to sit, the least important members of the household stood up to eat.

Beds were signs of status too. The older Shakespeare children would have slept in this bed, while any babies and younger children would have slept in the main bedroom. While the children who slept in this bed did not get a four-poster with a curtain round it to keep out the draughts, they did get to sleep in a real bed, unlike the apprentices.

The servants

Almost every household, except for the very poorest, had a servant or servants to help with the work. Mary Shakespeare would have had at least one young girl to help with the housework and cooking, probably two. These servants might have been local people, who did not neccesarily live in the Shakespeare household but were part of it, because they were there all day.

Apprentices

The Shakespeares probably had other people living with them too. Because John Shakespeare was a **craftsman**, he would have had one or two **apprentices** as part of his household. Apprentices were young boys who lived with a craftsman and were taught his craft. They had a contract with their master that said they had to work for him for free for a certain number of years, usually seven. In return, their master would teach them his craft and also feed, house and clothe them. When the seven years were up, the young man became a **journeyman**. This was someone who did not have his own business, but who was seen as being good at his craft. He had to work for another craftsman, but was paid wages for doing so. John Shakespeare might have employed a journeyman when business was especially good, but it is unlikely that he had enough business to employ one permanently as a part of the household.

Men

In **Tudor** society men were usually the head of the household. Depending on how important they were, men ran the family business, or went to work or, if the family was rich and important, went to the royal court. Although they were the most important person in the household they did not usually have anything to do with running the home. That was done by their wife or, if they had no wife, the most important woman in the household.

Men who had a trade, like John Shakespeare, usually worked from home. The unheated room at the end of the house was probably John's workshop (see the plan on page 29). It was separated from the rest of the house by a corridor that led to the garden at the back of the house. The window that faced onto the street was probably fitted with a shutter that hinged along the bottom of the window frame. The shutter could then be folded down to form a shop counter which opened onto the street. From here, John Shakespeare could talk to customers and other passers-by, and display his goods for sale – gloves, purses and belts. However, he probably did most of his trade on market days, when he and the other two master **glovers** of the town had permission to sell under the clock at the Market Cross, the best market site of all.

Gloves were made from animal skins. Deer and lambskin gloves were softer and more expensive than sheep or horseskin ones. Even more expensive were **kid** or goatskin gloves. John Shakespeare would have had to buy kid leather. To get from an animal skin to leather took several months.

Making gloves

Gloves were an important item in Tudor times. People wore them all the time, not just in winter to keep their hands warm. Gloves could be expensive and were often given as gifts. Glovers in London could make enough money to live well by just selling beautifully made gloves; sometimes scented or heavily decorated. In a small town like Stratford, glovers had to sell other small leather items too, such as belts and purses. They could not make shoes, however. Boot and shoe making was a separate craft.

Glovers had to work carefully, so they did not spoil the leather. They used very sharp scissors and knives (hanging up above the table) so as not to tear the leather. They also wetted the leather and stretched it to make shapes, such as a purse shape.

Finished gloves, purses and belts are on display in the workshop window. The window would have opened and acted as a counter for selling gloves.

Women

The women of Shakespeare's family ran the household. They cooked and cleaned, sewed and spun wool. All the jobs around the house took a long time – there was no modern machinery to make the work easier. In a large household the wife of the head of the household just gave the orders to a variety of servants, who then did the day-to-day work of running the home. All girls were expected to marry and raise a large family.

In the Shakespeare household, Mary Shakespeare would have done some of the work, although a servant would certainly have done the 'rough' jobs, such as scrubbing the floors and cleaning and lighting the fires. In most ordinary homes the women did a lot of **spinning**, weaving, knitting and sewing. In a family as well-off as the Shakespeares, the women probably did not make all the clothes, bedding and so on for the household. However, they would have made some of these things, especially as John Shakespeare traded in wool as well as leather goods.

The women sometimes did their spinning in the **parlour**. Once the wool was spun it was wound off the spinning wheel onto a wooden **skeiner** like the one shown here. The wool was wound tight onto the skeiner. When the skeiner was full, the wool was lifted off. Wool is stretchy, so when taken off the skeiner, the strands stopped being tight and twisted themselves around. The skeins that this made kept the wool neatly wound for storage.

Provisions

Women spent a lot of time buying, preparing and cooking food. Most fruit and vegetables were seasonal – there was a particular time of the year when they grew. When this time was passed, they could not be eaten again until the next year. Some meat was seasonal, too. Pigs were traditionally killed in the autumn, to save having to feed them through the winter, when there was far less food growing for animals and people. So women tried to preserve meat, fruit and vegetables in season so that there was more food for winter.

This is the larder of the Birthplace. Smoked meat was hung from hooks around the ceiling. Everything else was stored in pottery containers or barrels. You can see candles hanging in a bunch from the top shelf on the left. The women of the family might have made these themselves.

There were no freezers or fridges in the 16th century. Fresh food was kept in a **larder**, a room in the coolest part of the house with stone floors. However food went off much more quickly, especially in hot weather, so needed cooking in some way to preserve it. Fruits were made into jams and some vegetables were pickled and kept in sealed jars. Fruits were also carefully dried out and soaked in water before re-use.

Children

Childhood was dangerous in Shakespeare's age. Sickness and infection killed many more people then than it does today. Childbirth was a dangerous time for both babies and their mothers. The Shakespeares were quite a lucky family. Mary survived seven births and four of her children lived to grow up. In **Tudor** times it was not unusual for a man to marry several times because one or more wives died in childbirth.

Tiny adults

Tudor children were expected to grow up quickly. Babies and very young children had different kinds of clothes and ate different, very bland, food. However, from the age of about ten, children put their toys away. They wore adult clothes, ate adult food and were expected to begin to take part in the adult world, at whatever level in society their parents occupied. So boys of the Shakespeares level in society began to learn a trade, while girls learned to run a household.

Babies slept in wooden cradles, in the same room as their parents. Because they got dirtier than older children or adults, babies were bathed often – more times than Tudor people saw as 'normal', which was not very often at all! They were also bathed just after birth. Water was heated and then poured into a wooden bath, which was lined with a piece of cloth to keep the baby safe from splinters.

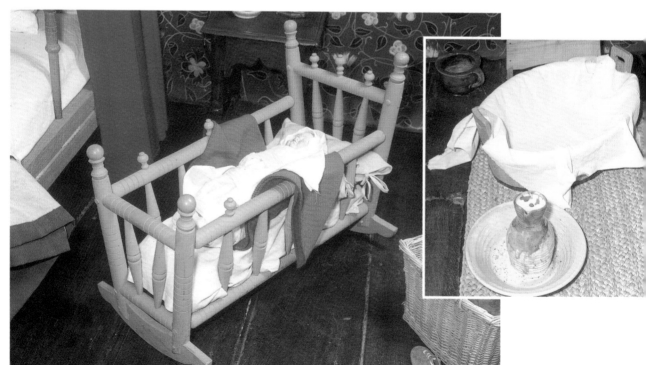

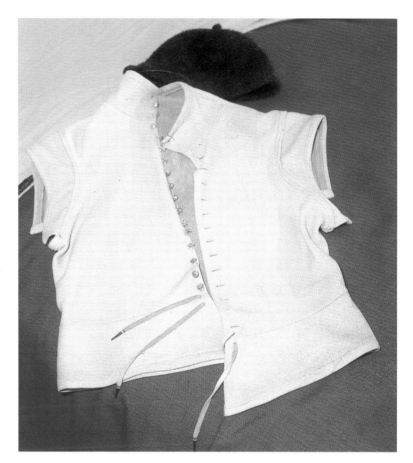

This is a modern version of a Tudor boy's leather jerkin, made to a Tudor pattern. Children did not have a separate style of dressing from adults once they stopped wearing the long robes that babies wore. They wore the same style of clothing as adults.

A changing view

The Shakespeare children were born at a time when ideas about who should be educated and what they should learn were changing. More and more books, plays and pamphlets were being written and English was taking off as a written language. As life became more complicated there was more need for people to have basic reading and writing skills.

Many schools had been set up, from 1500 on, to provide a basic education for the boys of tradesmen. They were taught **Latin** and ancient Greek as well as English, so that pupils could translate books, especially religious ones, only available in ancient languages. At this stage, Latin and Greek were the languages that were used in university and law schools. English was becoming used more often for books as well as ordinary writing, such as letters. The only other way to be educated was by expensive private lessons at home – something only the wealthy could provide for their children. John and Mary Shakespeare were not educated, but their boys certainly went to school. William left school with a sound knowledge of classical languages.

A special history

The Birthplace has been preserved because it is a very special place. It was bought in 1847 by a group of people (including the author Charles Dickens) who later set up a trust to preserve it for the nation.

More and more visitors

Between 1868 and 1869 the Birthplace had nearly 6000 visitors, about 1000 of them from the USA. The numbers have grown and grown. Even during the Second World War (1939–45), when normal life was torn apart, there were nearly 100,000 visitors a year.

The Shakespeare Birthplace Trust

In 1847 a committee was set up which became recognized as the Shakespeare Birthplace Trust in 1891. It took over the work of a body of concerned local people, because it was clear that it needed full-time management. Since this time the Trust has worked, with the help of many volunteers, to preserve the Birthplace while also giving as many people as possible the chance to visit.

This photo shows part of the Shakespeare Exhibition in the Birthplace.

New Place, the house that Shakespeare retired to from London, was pulled down in 1759, but the site was bought by the Shakespeare Birthplace Trust and turned into an Elizabethan garden. Nash's house can be seen on the left.

Continuing work

The Shakespeare Trust now looks after five houses associated with William Shakespeare: the Birthplace, Anne Hathaway's Cottage (where William Shakespeare's wife lived before her marriage to William), Mary Arden's House (where Shakespeare's mother grew up), Hall's Croft (where Shakespeare's daughter, Susanna went to live when she married Dr Hall) and New Place (the house that Shakespeare bought during his success in London, retired to and died in). They are continually working and researching to care for the properties and present them to visitors accurately.

In April 2000 the Trust re-opened the Birthplace, having represented it to fit the latest evidence about **Tudor** home furnishing and decoration. It also furnished John Shakespeare's workshop to show what it might have looked like. Original furniture and equipment have been used where possible. However, replica furniture, clothing, wall hangings, bedding and other equipment have been made to help to recreate the feel of the Birthplace. These have been carefully researched and made using Tudor materials and techniques. They give us a unique insight into daily life in Shakespeare's time.

Shakespeare is so famous that millions of tourists flock to Stratford to remember and learn about him. This monument to him was built beside the River Avon and, nearby, the Royal Shakespeare Theatre stages performances of his plays every year.

Timeline

About 1490	First house built on the Birthplace site in Henley Street, Stratford, part of a row of houses and shops
1552	John Shakespeare rents part of the Birthplace house in Henley Street
1556	John Shakespeare buys the Birthplace house in Henley Street
1564	William Shakespeare born in the Henley Street house
1575	John Shakespeare acquires adjacent property
1582	Shakespeare marries Anne Hathaway
1587	Shakespeare goes to live in London and starts to write plays and poems
1597	Shakespeare begins to buy land in and around Stratford
1601	John Shakespeare dies; William inherits the Birthplace. He has already bought himself a grand home in Stratford, New Place. Main house rented out to Lewis Hiccox, who turns it into an inn. Smaller house rented out to Shakespeare's sister Joan.
1847	The Birthplace bought from the widow of Thomas Court to be preserved for the nation. At this point it was run down and houses had been built onto either side, making it part of a terrace. A committee was set up which became recognized as the Shakespeare Birthplace Trust.
1857	Properties on either side of the Birthplace demolished, to reduce the risk of fire
1891	Shakespeare Birthplace Trust was formally acknowledged as managing the Birthplace. It also comes to care for four other houses that have close associations with William Shakespeare.
2000	The Birthplace represented to fit latest evidence about decoration and furnishing

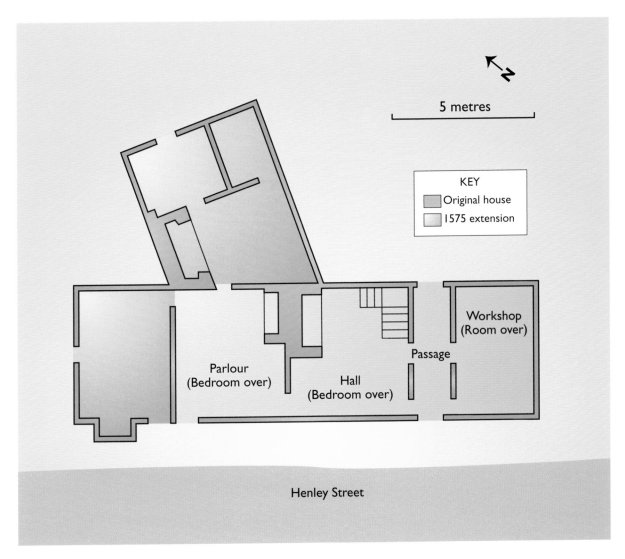

KEY
Original house
1575 extension

5 metres

Workshop
(Room over)

Passage

Parlour
(Bedroom over)

Hall
(Bedroom over)

Henley Street

Plan of Shakespeare's Birthplace.

Glossary

apprentice young person who agrees to work for nothing for someone who has a special skill, such as a builder, for several years. In return, they are fed, housed and taught a trade.

craftsman someone with a special skill that has to be learned, such as a builder or a glover

glover someone who makes gloves. In Shakespeare's time glovers would have worked with leather. Some glovers made nothing but gloves. Others also made small leather items such as purses and belts.

journeyman craftsman who has been an apprentice but has not yet set up his own business

kid young goat

larder cool room especially built as a food store

Latin language of the ancient Romans which was, in Shakespeare's time, the language that many books were written in

limewash mixture of lime (a powder made by burning rocks) and water. Limewash was painted onto walls because it was supposed to repel some kinds of insects.

linen cloth made from the stems of the flax plant

noble important, often wealthy person

parlour room that people used to sit and relax in

playwright person who writes plays – stories to be acted out

sewer special drain for getting rid of the waste from the toilet

size glue-like mixture, often made by boiling bones, used to stiffen fabric or paper

skeiner machine used to wind wool off the spinning wheel and twist it for storage

spinning taking fleece (wool cut from the back of the sheep), straightening out the fibres and twisting them, either by hand or on a machine called a spinning wheel, to make a woollen thread

spit long metal spike, held by metal supports on each end, put through pieces of meat so that they can be hung over a fire to cook

tapestry way of making cushions, curtains or wall hangings by stitching patterns onto a piece of cloth or stiffer cloth called canvas

Tudor the Tudor period was the time when the Tudor family ruled Britain. It lasted from 1485 to 1603. The Tudors were followed by the Stuart family. Shakespeare was born in the time of the last Tudor ruler, Queen Elizabeth I and died in the time of the first Stuart ruler, King James I.

wattle and daub flexible sticks (wattle) woven into panels to fill the space between the wooden beams in buildings. These panels were then covered in a layer of mud and straw (daub).

Index

Titles in the *Visiting the past* series include:

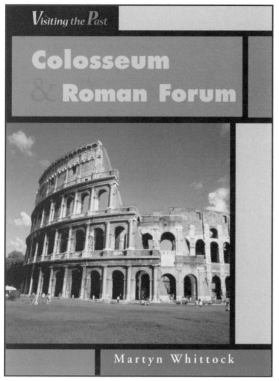

Hardback   0 431 02786 2

Hardback   0 431 02787 0

Hardback   0 431 02784 6

Hardback   0 431 02785 4

Find out about the other titles in this series on our website www.heinemann.co.uk/library